THE CHRISTMAS TREE FARM

Adam Szymkowicz

BROADWAY PLAY PUBLISHING INC
New York
www.broadwayplaypublishing.com
info@broadwayplaypublishing.com

Cover photo: David White Studio

First edition: May 2024
I S B N: 979-8-88856-015-0

Book design: Marie Donovan
Page make-up: Adobe InDesign
Typeface: Palatino

For Nandita Shenoy who every year tells me what
Christmas movies to watch. You are a great friend and
an amazing artist. Thank you for being in my plays.

and

For Kevin R Free, an uber talented human I get to call
friend. Thank you for programming this play and
taking a chance on me.

THE CHRISTMAS TREE FARM premiered at Mile Square Theater (Kevin R Free, Artistic Director) in Hoboken, NJ opening on 30 November 2023. The cast and creative contributors were:

BRI .... Nandita Shenoy
Actor 2 .... Keivana Wallace
Actor 3 ....Sarah Elizabeth Grace
Actor 4 ....Aaron Parker Fouhey
Actor 5 ....Nathaniel Kent

Director ....Rachel Dart
Stage Manager ....Arielle Legere
Production Manager ....Jen Price Fick
Assistant Stage Manager .... Melissa John
Scenic design ....Court Watson
Costume design .... Alicia J Austin
Lighting design .... Victoria Bain
Associate lighting design .... Aaron Tacy
Property design & scenic painting .... Em Grosland
Sound design .... D J Potts
Music Director .... Jeff Ostermueller
Technical Director ....Nate Hamm
Scenic / prop overhire ....Sophie Chaves Gamboa, Tais Fontanez, Leon Valencia
Production Electrician .... Ian Lloyd Sanchez
Electricians ....Nick Meittinis, Lara Kling
Wardrobe .... Jasmin Casiano
Publicity/production photos .... David White Studio
House & Box Office Manager ....Leon Valencia
Video promo ....Branding Shorts
Front of house ....Tais Fontanez, Rossella Lopez, Ian Lloyd Sanchez, Jasmin Casiano

THE CHRISTMAS TREE FARM was subsequently produced at Actors Bridge Ensemble (Vali Forrister, Producer) in Nashville, TN, opening on 15 December 2023. The cast and creative contributors were:

BRI .... Josh Inocalla
RED (*now* FRITO) .... Caroline Conner
RUTABAGA .... Sofia Apuzzo
SANTA 1 .... Scott Patrick Wilson
SANTA 2 .... Betsy Black
SANTA 3 .... Sally Bebawy
Santa 4 .... Bob Locknar
ELF .... Carolyn Carter
TERRY .... Scott Patrick Wilson
A.E. .... Stacey Hucks
E.A. .... Rebecca Scarpati
RIVER .... Sofia Apuzzo
TAYLOR .... Betsy Black
DIRECTOR .... Rebecca Scarpati
BUSY CAREER WOMAN .... Carolyn Carter
DASHING HANDSOME MAN .... Natalie Tita
ANGEL .... Scott Patrick Wilson
QUINN .... Stacey Hucks
PALMER .... Bob Locknar
DREW .... Natalie Tita
J .... Sally Bebawy
DANA .... Caroline Conner

Director .... Vali Forrister
Stage Manager .... Kat Tierney-Smith
Scenic Designer .... Paul Gatrell
Lighting Designer .... Richard Davis, LC, MIES
Costume Designer .... Dee Benn
Photographer .... Sally Bebawy Photography

SPECIAL THANKS

To the phenomenal Rachel Dart and the amazing cast and crew at Mile Square. And the great Kevin R Free.

Kip and Michael at BPPI.

Thanks to DJ for identifying the correct place for the third angelic sound.

Vali and her group at Actors Bridge.

Kathleen Gilbert Switzer and her group at El Dorado High School.

Thanks to Seth Glewen and everyone at Gersh. Lily Creed. Vern Co. Ethan Harari. John and Rhoda Szymkowicz. Kristen Palmer. Wallace Szymkowicz. Kelly Jean Fitzsimmons. The Juilliard School. Betty and David Michel.

Corrina Schulenburg, Sienna Gonzalez and everyone at Flux Core. Heather Cohn. Mercena Schulenburg for starting a standing ovation. Kelly O'Donnell, Nandita Shenoy, Alisha Spielmann, Ryan Vincent Anderson, Matthew Trumbull, Jessica Angleskhan, Emily Ma. Project Y, Lia Romeo and Liz Appel, Eleanor Burgess, Mathilde Dratwa, Enid Graham, Mary Elizabeth Hamilton, Ying Ying Li, Erin Mallon, Deepa Purohit, Deneen Reynolds-Knott.

Ellen Morrone. Judy Landman. Emily Rubin. Lindsey Buller Maliekel and Joe Maliekel. David White Studio. Susan Weiss. Tish Dace.

Gwydion Suilebhan and The New Play Exchange. Samantha Marchant, Claudia Haas, Glenn Morehouse Olson, Aly Kantor, Nora Louise Syran, Stephen Kaplan.

Mark and David and Milanovich and everyone at The Drama Book Shop.

CHARACTERS

5-21 actors. At least 1M, 1F, 3 any gender.

Many of these are love stories. Queer love stories are encouraged. I wanted to leave it open as much as I could for you to use the actors you have available. So I tried to leave gender open when possible. Please cast with an eye towards diversity in all senses of the word, to best portray your community. But also do this in a thoughtful way. There are lots of tensions and power structures out in the world. Be careful not to contribute to any stereotypes inadvertently by your casting choices. When in the script, you see (he/she/them, etc) that means you fill in the appropriate pronoun.

ONE "Welcome"

BRI, *any gender,* BRI *could be short for Brian or Brianna or BringMeAFiggyPudding. Dressed like a farmer but a chic farmer who deals with customers.* BRI *is in every scene.*

TWO "Meet Cute"

FRITO, *any gender, around the same age as* RUTABAGA
RUTABAGA, *any gender, around the same age as* FRITO

THREE "Four Santas"

SANTA 1, *any gender, dressed like Santa Claus*
SANTA 2, *any gender, dressed like Santa Claus*

SANTA 3, *any gender, dressed like Santa Claus*
SANTA 4, *any gender, dressed like Santa Claus*

FOUR "Elf"

ELF, *any gender, dressed as an elf*

FIVE "Terry"

TERRY, *any gender, young or around the same age as* BRI

SIX "The Novelists"

A.E., *any gender, Literary, around the same age as* E.A.
E.A., *any gender, Literary, around the same age as* A.E.

SEVEN "Stargazing"

RIVER, *any gender, a young adult*
TAYLOR, *any gender, a young adult*

EIGHT "Christmas Movie"

DIRECTOR, *any gender*
BUSY CAREER WOMAN, *female*
DASHING HANDSOME MAN, *male*
ANGEL, *any gender, angelic*

NINE "High School Sweethearts"

QUINN, *any gender, around the same age as* PALMER
PALMER, *any gender, around the same age as* QUINN

TEN "Garden Center Visit"
DREW, *any gender, around the same age as* BRI
TERRY, *any gender, young or around the same age as* BRI

ELEVEN "The Perfect Tree"
J, *male, young*

TWELVE "Tree Lighting"
DANA, *female, the mayor*

SETTING

A small New England town. A Christmas tree farm. In other words, the stage is full of trees spaced equally apart. A small table or stand where BRI *takes payment, offers refreshments.*

This could also be staged outside at an actual farm. A bare stage is also possible.

Time: Nowish, November or December

NOTES

Avoid blackouts. Best to keep it moving.
Running time: about 75-85 minutes

ONE
"Welcome"

(Carolers made up of the entire cast except for BRI *sing Christmas carols. Lots of Christmas carols are in the public domain. This caroling can happen as the audience comes in if you like. If not, maybe only sing one song—Deck the Halls or O' Christmas Tree.)*

(They finish and BRI *applauds.)*

BRI: That was great! Thanks for stopping by. Anyone need a tree still? Also got some popcorn, hot cider. Hot chocolate. Yeah, please help yourself. Good to see you.

(They mill around and finally file out.)

BRI: *(To audience)* Hi. I'm Bri. This is my place. The Lake Hayward Christmas Tree Farm. Really we're only busy for a few weeks a year. Yeah you could go to the Garden Center and get a tree that's already been cut. They get them from Canada I think but these ones grow right here. I planted them. That probably counts for something. I know people like artificial trees because they don't like to water them or clean up needles but my industry—I'm a small part of this industry—my industry is actually more eco friendly. We grow three hundred and fifty million trees every year. That's a lot of oxygen we put in the air. Only about thirty million or so are cut down each year. And look at them. They're beautiful, biodegradable. They smell good. Might make you feel good too. Or if you have a cat? I bet your cats love it too. And you could support my small business.

A couple guidelines. If you see a tree with a tag on it, that means someone already reserved it and will come get it later. Don't cut down a tree that has a tag on it. Once you pick out your perfect tree, you can cut it down yourself or come get me and I'll cut it for you. I can help tie it to your car too if you want. That's about it. You need help, just holler. I'm Bri.

Oh and, maybe this goes without saying but Christmas tree farms are kind of magical places. My advice is stay open to the magic that can happen in such a setting. Like for example. Right now there's a meet cute maybe happening.

TWO
"Meet Cute"

(FRITO *and* RUTABAGA *circling a tree.*)

FRITO: Oh did you?

RUTABAGA: What?

FRITO: Was this your tree?

RUTABAGA: No. Kind of. No. You want it?

FRITO: No. Yes. It's a nice tree.

RUTABAGA: It is. There are others though. I don't need this one.

FRITO: But you want it.

RUTABAGA: But I want it.

FRITO: You can have it.

RUTABAGA: No. You take it.

FRITO: You were probably here first.

RUTABAGA: Do I even need a tree this year?

FRITO: I mean, I'm going to get one. It doesn't have to be this one. I could get that one over there.

RUTABAGA: You like that one?

FRITO: No. But I haven't looked at them all.

RUTABAGA: I have. I looked at them all. This is the best one.

FRITO: Oh. Well then you should have it. I don't need the best. I just want something nice. Really it's about the lights and the ornaments anyway.

RUTABAGA: I didn't mean to imply I need the best of everything. I'm not that person. I like nice things okay but— Why am I saying this? I may not even get a tree this year.

FRITO: Why?

RUTABAGA: I'm all alone this year. Who will even see it besides me?

FRITO: I'm sorry you're all alone.

RUTABAGA: I'm not all alone. I have friends. I just mean. It's just me in the house. Sorry. Who are you? Do we know each other?

FRITO: No. I've seen you around, I think. Hi. I'm Frito.

RUTABAGA: Frito, is that your real name?

FRITO: It's kind of just what people call me.

RUTABAGA: You work at the—

FRITO: Yeah.

RUTABAGA: Right. Hi. I'm Rue.

FRITO: That your real name?

RUTABAGA: Yeah.

FRITO: I like it. It suits you.

RUTABAGA: It's short for…never mind.

FRITO: What?

RUTABAGA: Rutabaga. My parents, they were, there's no accounting for why they named me Rutabaga.

FRITO: I like it.

RUTABAGA: Well yeah. I've come around to it again. Anyway, my mom died last year.

FRITO: I'm sorry.

RUTABAGA: Thanks, yeah. And my dad died when I was in college. So I'm wondering who is the tree even for. We used to decorate it together. But now that she's not here…

FRITO: I get it. It's still nice though. To take the time to put up a tree and decorate it.

RUTABAGA: Trim it.

FRITO: Yeah, why do they call it that? Trimming the tree?

RUTABAGA: I don't know. Are we supposed to prune it?

FRITO: I don't think so.

RUTABAGA: You take it. I'm just going to go home.

FRITO: No. You have it.

RUTABAGA: I'm just not going to do a tree this year I think.

FRITO: That'd be a shame.

RUTABAGA: It's a thing to do with other people.

FRITO: I could…I'm sorry never mind.

RUTABAGA: You could what?

FRITO: If this is too forward, please… but I could help you decorate your tree.

RUTABAGA: Oh.

FRITO: If I'm honest, I've seen you around.

RUTABAGA: Yeah.

FRITO: And I've wondered about you.

RUTABAGA: Oh?

FRITO: I'm not trying to —It would be like getting coffee except it's decorating a tree instead.

RUTABAGA: In my home.

FRITO: Well, yeah. Sorry, you're right.

RUTABAGA: I've seen you around too.

FRITO: Really?

RUTABAGA: Well yeah, you work at the—

FRITO: Right.

RUTABAGA: You're friends with Tyler.

FRITO: Yeah.

RUTABAGA: Tyler's a real good person.

FRITO: Yeah.

RUTABAGA: Are you?

FRITO: What?

RUTABAGA: A good person?

FRITO: I try.

RUTABAGA: That's not nothing. Some people don't try. Some people revel in the opposite.

FRITO: Yeah. I don't like that.

RUTABAGA: No. You want to decorate a tree with me, huh?

FRITO: You ever done that?

RUTABAGA: When I was with someone, sure. Of course. I was—I mean things were serious once.

FRITO: Oh.

RUTABAGA: You ever been—

FRITO: Serious? Sure. And then we weren't anymore. For a long time too. I thought… but no. Here I am all alone getting a tree.

RUTABAGA: The thing is, I don't think you can just casually decorate a tree. It's memory building, you know, taking the ornaments passed down by your parents or given to you when you were a child. And there's expectations of other activities too.

FRITO: Oh, I didn't mean that.

RUTABAGA: Baking maybe. Gingerbread or heating up milk for cocoa. It's not like going for coffee for fifteen minutes and someone can walk out if it doesn't feel right.

FRITO: Yeah, no. I don't know what I was thinking.

RUTABAGA: And there's the baggage too. From the times before. The accumulation of rejections and failure. The hope of new love and the inevitable crushing depression from love lost. And you start to think, well, maybe it's just not for me. Maybe I'm not someone who can ever be happy in that way. Not that that's the only way to be happy. It's just— Love like that has always been something I wanted for me. My parents were happy in love, most of the time so maybe that's why or else it's just always been bad timing. But when years of loneliness build on years of loneliness, it's hard to shake that off. It takes a lot to hope again.

FRITO: Okay, well I get that. Maybe we could try that fifteen minutes of coffee instead sometime where one of us walks out?

(*A beat.* FRITO *and* RUTABAGA *look at each other.* BRI *enters.*)

BRI: (*Entering*) See anything you like?

RUTABAGA: Yeah. I do actually. I see something that could maybe be something. Maybe. I hope. We'll take this one.

FRITO: We?

RUTABAGA: We're going to trim it together.

THREE
"Four Santas"

BRI: People congregate at my farm sometimes. I try to make it welcoming this time of year. Today four Santas came to the farm after their shifts.

(Enter four SANTA CLAUSES *drinking eggnog from travel mugs.)*

SANTA 3: *(Creepy to* SANTA 2*)* I see you when you're sleeping.

SANTA 2: Stop it! You're being creepy.

SANTA 3: *(Creepy, still)* I know when you're awake.

SANTA 2: Noo!

SANTA 3: You're on my list!

SANTA 2: Stop!

SANTA 1: I now call to order this annual meeting of area Santas.

SANTA 2, SANTA 3, SANTA 4: Ho. Ho. Ho.

SANTA 1: We have descended on this Christmas tree farm to find the true meaning of Christmas

SANTA 3: No!

SANTA 1: What?

SANTA 4: We aren't doing that.

SANTA 1: Yes we are. We must compete to find the truest expression of what Christmas means.

SANTA 4: No. That didn't go well last time. You remember.

SANTA 1: I just thought this year—

SANTA 4: No competition.

SANTA 1: Then what are we doing here?

SANTA 2: We just thought it would be nice.

SANTA 3: It is nice.

SANTA 2: Right? We'll hang out. Talk. No pressure.

SANTA 1: Sure but maybe a competition would make it better.

SANTA 2: Just take a breath. Breathe in the fresh air. Appreciate being here.

SANTA 1: Yeah I am. I'm just saying.

SANTA 4: No. Not happening.

BRI: Let me get you oriented. (*About* SANTAS 1, 2, 3.) Santa is in love with Santa who is in love with Santa who maybe is only in love with (*himself/herself/themself, etc. About* SANTA 4) Santa on the other hand hasn't been in love with anyone for ten years or so. They all love Christmas. And children. Santa never had any children of (*his/her/their*) own. Santa's children are grown. Santa and Santa dated elves in the past, but this year they have not brought any elves with them here to this, a sacred place.
They are all…a little lonely. They drink their egg nog. They look at the trees.

SANTA 2: I want to say something. I know the daily grind of photos and laps can be hard so I thought, let's come back here to help us remember what we're doing it all for.

SANTA 3: Are you going to talk about the manger?

SANTA 1: Or the true meaning of Christmas?

SANTA 2: No, I wasn't going to.

SANTA 1: I just want to say—

SANTA 4: No.

SANTA 1: No but I just want to say—

SANTA 4: No!

SANTA 1: —The true meaning of Christmas is finding the generosity inside yourself you didn't know was there.

SANTA 4: Oh. That's okay.

SANTA 3: I appreciate that.

SANTA 1: The children can be sticky and smelly and sometimes wet. They need us. They believe in us. And I think we believe in them too.

SANTA 2: Yeah. That's nice.

SANTA 3: It's helpful to remember about generosity after you've been peed on for the third time in an hour.

SANTA 1: Exactly. So did I win?

SANTA 4: It's not a competition.

SANTA 1: But it could be.

SANTA 2: When I was a kid, every year my dad would take us to the woods and we'd cut down our own tree. It was the most magical part of Christmas for me.

SANTA 3: More magical than lights?

SANTA 4: Or presents?

SANTA 1: Or cookies?

SANTA 3: Or tinsel. Don't you find tinsel really magical?

SANTA 2: Kind of. Putting the tree up was always hard for some reason. There was shouting and frustration. The cat might knock it over. It was difficult to get it in the house. Every year my dad would yell in the middle

of all the chaos, "We're not getting a tree next year!"
But then the next year would come and we'd all bundle
up and march out into the woods behind him, pick out
a tree too big for our house again. I don't know. I miss
my dad. Maybe that's why I dress up like this every
year.

SANTA 4: I'm just a Christmas addict. I love it all.

SANTA 3: Yeah, we know.

SANTA 4: You got to come see my train table. I got some
new parts of the village. It's real magical.

SANTA 2: We'll come see it.

SANTA 3: Yeah, we will. For me it was when I was in
my accident.

SANTA 2: Your near death experience?

SANTA 3: Yeah. I was trapped in my car, upside down,
half dead and an angel appeared to me.

SANTA 1: It was probably an EMT.

SANTA 3: No, it was an angel.

SANTA 4: What did she say?

SANTA 3: She said, "It's not too late to turn your life
around."

SANTA 4: Did you? Turn your life around?

SANTA 3: Is what you see a turned-around-life? No.
Maybe. There have been strong improvements. Lots of
ups and downs. Anyway, I started playing Santa after
the accident.

SANTA 1: Okay, well. If we're not going to name a
winner, are we done here?

SANTA 2: I want to stay a little longer.

SANTA 3: I'll stay.

SANTA 1: Fine!

SANTA 4: I feel like I should say something even though I probably shouldn't say anything.

SANTA 1: What?

SANTA 4: There's been a vibe this year. Certain Santas amongst us have feelings I think for certain other Santas.

SANTA 3: Wait, really?

SANTA 4: Nobody has to say anything if they don't want to but maybe you should look in your heart and see if there's any room in there for anyone here. I'm not talking about me. This isn't about me. I'm not—I don't know if I can ever love again. But you folks, well if you can, you should, if it's right. I don't know.

SANTA 1: I must admit, I do have feelings.

SANTA 2: Oh, you're looking at me.

SANTA 1: Yeah.

SANTA 2: I haven't thought of you like that.

SANTA 1: Could you?

SANTA 2: Sorry. The thing is I kind of have other feelings.

SANTA 3: You're looking at me.

SANTA 2: Am I? I guess I am.

SANTA 3: I haven't thought about you like that.

SANTA 2: Could you?

SANTA 3: Maybe. Wow. Really? What do you like about me most?

(SANTA 2 *and* SANTA 3 *exit arm in arm.*)

SANTA 4: Sorry about that.

SANTA 1: It's okay.

SANTA 4: I didn't really know which way that would go but I thought it could use a push.

SANTA 1: At least now I know.

SANTA 4: Better than never knowing.

SANTA 1: Maybe. Hey, what's your deal?

SANTA 4: It's just been a while since there's been anyone I'm interested in.

SANTA 1: I've never been like that. I have so many crushes.

SANTA 4: That's nice.

SANTA 1: It would be if one worked out. Although I also just like to think about them sometimes. Makes the day go by faster. The longing. Bittersweet. Course right now it's just pain.

SANTA 4: I wish there was something I could do to make you feel better. Candy cane?

(SANTA 1 *accepts the candy cane, unwraps to eat.*)

SANTA 4: What do you think? Can you stand to hang out a while longer?

SANTA 1: It hurts. But I'm going to lead with generosity.

SANTA 4: That's the spirit.

SANTA 1: We should go see the lights on the green.

SANTA 4: They're not up yet.

SANTA 1: We'll have to come back.

BRI: Are you leaving already? Anyone want a tree?

SANTA 4: I'll be back tomorrow, Bri. You have a good holiday.

BRI: You too!

SANTA 1: Merry Christmas!

(*Exit* SANTA 4 *and* SANTA 1.)

BRI: The number of Santas attending meetings increases the next few years.
There are six, then eight, then fifteen until they dwindle again. Eventually there are only two who keep coming back every year to remember.

FOUR
"Elf"

BRI: Over the years, I've seen lots of important moments. I see couples getting their first trees, couples getting their last trees. I see non-Christian kids lobbying for Christmas trees and by extension, Christmas presents. I see people showing up in blizzards to get a tree the day before Christmas. Families picking out trees together year after year. You watch kids grow up and sometimes they come here as adults with their families too. Or they come back for the sleigh rides. Sometimes we hold a snowman building competition. Or they go skating on the lake and come by to say hi. People I've known my whole life. It was a family farm and now it's my farm. I don't know if I'll have kids but maybe I'll pass it down someday too.

(*Enter* ELF.)

ELF: Hey!

BRI: Oh, Hi. Help you find a tree?

ELF: No, I was looking for—

BRI: The Santas have come and gone. But I'm sure you'll catch your Santa back at work.

ELF: Right. Yeah, right. I guess I wasn't actually invited this time.

BRI: Oh, I'm sorry.

ELF: Not your fault.

BRI: I should tell you, I don't think it's going to happen this year, with you and Santa.

ELF: Oh. Yeah. I guess I kind of knew that, actually. But it helps to hear someone say it out loud.

BRI: It just wasn't a good match, maybe.

ELF: I know. I mean I knew that I guess.

BRI: Or it's the timing. So much is about timing.

ELF: Right. I really want a date for New Years though.

BRI: Oh.

ELF: There's a party. And I can't stand to be alone again this year.

BRI: I understand.

ELF: What about you?

BRI: Me?

ELF: You free on New Years?

BRI: Oh, I'm flattered but…

ELF: You have other plans?

BRI: Well, no. I guess I don't.

ELF: You don't have to work. Not here anyway. No one buying a tree on New Years.

BRI: I suppose not. But I usually get invited somewhere.

ELF: Right. I'm inviting you right now.

BRI: Thanks, that's—but—I guess if I'm honest, my heart belongs to someone else.

ELF: Oh. Yeah mine probably does too. But we could still have a good time.

BRI: Uh. I'll think about it.

ELF: Yeah. Let me know if you change your mind.

BRI: I will. Maybe this year… You want a tree?

ELF: Yeah, I'll go take a look. You have a special discount for people you're considering going on a date with?

BRI: I just might.

(*Exit* ELF.)

BRI: I just might.

FIVE
"Terry"

BRI: And then around dusk, Terry is there.

(*Enter* TERRY *who probably wears pale or white clothes. Leather jacket also possible.*)

TERRY: Hey!

BRI: Terry! It seems like I always see you around this time of year.

TERRY: You look good.

BRI: You look the same. You want to come inside for a minute?

TERRY: Nah.

BRI: Are you cold? Do you get cold?

TERRY: I'm fine. The cold suits me.

BRI: You come to see me?

TERRY: Sometimes I just like to go where it's quiet.

BRI: Super mysterious, Terry.

TERRY: Nah.

BRI: But I guess it's real quiet here.

TERRY: Out here amongst the trees, yeah. I bet it helps you quiet your mind too.

BRI: Maybe a bit. But I'm doing okay. Definitely better than when I was younger. I was a nervous kid.

TERRY: No. Were you?

BRI: You know I was.

TERRY: I didn't think about you like that.

BRI: You thought about me though? In high school. I mean of course you did. We were friends. I just mean— I don't know what I mean. You know what I mean.

TERRY: I like the look of this winter sky, even when it's gray day after gray day. It's like a Swedish film.

BRI: When you would talk this way, I used to think it was a kind of poetry.

TERRY: What do you think now?

BRI: Does it even matter?

TERRY: What mood is this? Are you being nostalgic or melancholy?

BRI: What is it called when you yearn for a time long gone even though you know you're happier now.

TERRY: I'm glad you're doing well.

BRI: I am. I really am. I mean not everything's perfect I guess but whose life is? I used to—no, never mind.

TERRY: You can say anything. It's just you and me.

BRI: I guess it doesn't matter much anymore but I was madly in love with you when we were young

TERRY: I mean I guess I wondered about that.

BRI: And I always wondered what you felt about me— Did you ever think about me when I wasn't around?

TERRY: I thought about lots of things and people.

BRI: Yeah, It does't feel so much like poetry now.

TERRY: Sorry. I guess—

BRI: You here for any reason?

TERRY: You find a silver lighter out here? I can't seem to find it.

BRI: Oh, your lighter. I forgot about your ever present lighter. No, I haven't seen anything like that. Things get buried easily though out here.

TERRY: All right then. I'm off.

BRI: Going so soon? When will I see you again?

TERRY: I don't know.

BRI: Will you be at the Christmas tree lighting?

TERRY: Maybe. Nah. I don't know. Take care of yourself. *(Exits)*

BRI: And he's gone. *(Looks down. Picks up a silver zippo lighter off the ground.)* Wait! Terry!? ...But he's gone. *(She fiddles with the lighter.)* And I wonder. Then I make myself stop wondering.

SIX
"The Novelists"

BRI: The novelists walk through the rows of trees. E.A. and A.E. A.E. and E.A. Married for...well, it's been twenty something years. I could look it up. Anyway, it's not been an insignificant amount of time.

A.E.: You really want a tree this year?

E.A.: Thinking about it.

A.E.: Even though you're Jewish?

E.A.: Even though you're agnostic. We've had trees before.

A.E.: When the kids were in the house.

E.A.: It's nice though, right? All lit up?

A.E.: It is.

BRI: They think about when the kids were in the house. The menorah in one window, the Christmas tree in the other. The presents. The energy. The crying and laughing. The endless noise and trash. They miss it.

E.A.: But probably you're right. We don't need a tree.

A.E.: I didn't say that.

BRI: There's a delightful crunch underfoot as they walk through the frosty paths of Douglas Firs. They are lost in their own thoughts. A.E. thinks of outdoor adventure, survival, endurance. E.A. wonders how to start a difficult conversation.

A.E.: Did you see the snowflake?

E.A.: What?

A.E.: I thought I saw a snowflake for a second.

E.A.: No. No. I didn't see it.

A.E.: I swear I saw a snowflake just now.

BRI: A silence descends. How to describe such a silence? E.A and A.E describe silences differently in their books. Usually A.E. describes the physical sensation, or the facial expression or the visual impact of the task at hand. E.A.'s go-to is the internal monologue.

E.A.: *(Internal monologue)* How to— How to begin— You have to jump in feet first or headfirst even and then let the rest sort itself out. You remember when you were young and fell into love completely. Your head buzzing with all those sweet chemicals, your blood pounding at every embrace. You were in it so you just said yes and and yes and stumbled blind into your future. Well that's what you have to do again. Don't dither. Be bold and hope for the best. It's the only way.

A.E.: What are you thinking about?

E.A.: The thing I'm writing.

A.E.: Are you struggling?

E.A.: I might be struggling.

A.E.: You always figure it out.

E.A.: I do, don't I?

A.E.: We both do.

E.A.: Our capacity for figuring things out is admirable. So is our ability to deal with big changes.

A.E.: What changes?

E.A.: I didn't bring you here to get a Christmas tree. I came here to talk about divorce.

A.E.: Oh. What? Our divorce?

E.A.: Indeed.

A.E.: You think we should get divorced.

E.A.: That's what I've been thinking.

A.E.: Have you been thinking about this long?

E.A.: Not long, no.

BRI: But that's not entirely true. Once about three years into the marriage, E.A. thought about it a lot for a short time. And then on a periodic basis during the last five years, *(he/she/they)* wrote lists and plans, schedules, eventualities. Maybe *(he/she/they)* worked on separation possibilities more than anything else. The charts alone took up almost a whole wall.

A.E.: I must admit I did not see this coming.

E.A.: It's nothing personal.

A.E.: No?

Bri: How could it not be personal?

E.A.: It's nothing you did.

Bri: It's a thousand little things.

E.A.: I'm just not sure about you anymore.

Bri: This hits home. There are times in a relationship when the ugliness of who you can be sneaks out and, once seen, it can never be unseen. Some people are good at forgetting or forgiving, at small kindnesses. Other people are good at hiding who they really are maybe. It's all about what you're willing to live with. And who you can love. And what kind of hurt can break the bonds of love. For them, it wasn't one big thing, but a collection of weights that tipped the scale over time. The erosion of a mountain is just one drop of rain over and over. So it's maybe a surprise but it shouldn't be a surprise.

A.E.: You're sick of me.

E.A.: Maybe.

A.E.: I didn't think we'd ever get sick of each other. I didn't think our relationship would ever crumble. Or rather I imagined it happening many times but I never believed it. This is what happens to other people.

E.A.: So many of our friends are divorced now.

A.E.: Yeah. It was like a disease for a while, creeping from house to house. And I thought, well, we escaped that, but now—

E.A.: Sometimes there's no escape.

Bri: They both think of how they will write about this. The world will maybe get two good novels because of this conversation.

A.E.: Should I move out?

E.A.: Yes. Do you mind?

A.E.: Of course I mind. But I'll do it.

E.A.: Will you move to Poughkeepsie?

A.E.: I might, yeah. Or back to the city. No. Maybe. I don't know. Oh! I'll have to start dating.

E.A.: You don't have to do anything.

A.E.: Maybe it's for the best.

E.A.: I think it is. Thank you. For moving out.

A.E.: I guess I'll start packing.

E.A.: Not yet. After the holiday, okay.

A.E.: Okay. Do you hate me?

E.A.: I don't hate you.

A.E.: I'm starting to hate you a little. *(beat)* Are you sure? Are you sure we're done.

E.A.: You think you can talk me out of this still.

A.E.: No. I don't. I don't know.

E.A.: We should get a tree. Our last tree.

A.E.: I'd like that actually.

BRI: Afterwards, they separate out their ornaments into two boxes. Like everything else in the house. Commingled for so long that it's hard to know what belongs to whom. But life moves on even if your former spouse has the only potato peeler. And right now—

A.E.: There. Did you see that snowflake? You must have seen that one.

E.A.: No. I missed it.

SEVEN
"Stargazing"

BRI: Nighttime.

(The stars come out. Enter RIVER *and* TAYLOR.*)*

(They may stand with a blanket behind them as if they're lying down on it and we in the audience are the sky they're gazing at.)

BRI: They think I don't know they do it, but a young couple, Taylor and River come to my farm and lie on the grass between the trees to look at the stars. Usually they remember to bring a blanket. They come for the meteor showers and to watch the international space station pass. But they also come just to look at the night sky. Our sky is really big here on the farm. The more silent the night, the more that is said in the dark between them, so when they do speak—

RIVER: Oh. Look at that.

BRI: They are able to say things that are harder to say in the daylight to another person's face. Especially when that face belongs to someone you're all tangled up in. But in the dark it's easier to say things like—

TAYLOR: I'm afraid of becoming like my father.

RIVER: That will never happen.

BRI: And.

RIVER: We should get a dog. I want a place with a backyard so we can have a dog.

TAYLOR: What kind?

RIVER: I like lots of kinds. What kind do you like?

TAYLOR: One of those huge ones that dig skiers out of avalanches.

RIVER: Okay.

TAYLOR: Like almost the size of the small horse. If I hurt my leg, I could ride it to the grocery store.

RIVER: I have a car.

TAYLOR: Okay but it needs to be big enough to fit our dog in it.

RIVER: We're gonna need a bigger car. Unless you ride the dog everywhere.

TAYLOR: I'm not—I don't think I'll really do that.

BRI: And.

TAYLOR: Do you believe in ghosts.

RIVER: Yeah I do.

TAYLOR: What about angels?

RIVER: Why do you ask?

TAYLOR: I think I saw something.

RIVER: Your grandmother?

TAYLOR: No. I don't know.

BRI: And.

RIVER: Do you think I'm a good person?

TAYLOR: Of course.

RIVER: I'm not so sure.

TAYLOR: You're trying to be better. That's what's important.

RIVER: I could try harder.

BRI: And.

TAYLOR: Is the important thing service to others? Like is that what we're here to do?

BRI: And.

RIVER: Do you ever think while we're lying here aliens may swoop down and abduct us?

TAYLOR: Don't say that.

BRI: And.

RIVER: We all change, but what if I change too much in the wrong ways?

TAYLOR: That could happen. But then you could just change again.

RIVER: But what if I can't? You could get sick of me.

TAYLOR: Let's just look at the stars, okay?

BRI: So they do. Night after night. This night, Taylor looks at Orion's Belt and says

TAYLOR: What if I never amount to anything? Some days everything seems possible and other days nothing seems to happen. Look at this tiny piece of universe we get to see. Does anything matter?

RIVER: We decide what matters. Right now we're the only ones alive on this earth. No one else's opinion matters. No one is here but you and me.

BRI: In ten years they will bring their child out here to look at the stars with them. But right now, River has something to say.

RIVER: I need to tell you something.

BRI: Taylor is suddenly afraid.

TAYLOR: Is it—

RIVER: I got into Cal Arts!

TAYLOR: You did!? That's great! That's great.

RIVER: Will you go with me?

TAYLOR: What will I do there? It's across the country. Do they have the same stars there?

RIVER: I need you there. You're everything.

TAYLOR: I'm not everything.

RIVER: You're a lot.

TAYLOR: I have to think. It's scary. It's the future. No one knows what will happen.

BRI: The future has a funny way of becoming the past. Time passes in an instant. They grow older. Their children grow up. River's mom dies. The other parents follow. Teachers, coaches, pets—that big dog they loved, eventually they must mourn them all. Then they are old themselves. One day they are too old to lie on the ground and look at the stars. But not today.

TAYLOR: I'll go with you. If you're sure that's what you want.

RIVER: I'm sure. The only thing I'm sure about is you.

TAYLOR: I'm sure about you too.

EIGHT
"Christmas Movie"

BRI: So if you know me at all, you know I love films. In fact, once I thought I'd be more involved in that world. The path not taken. Anyway, I'm very excited when a filmmaker comes to my tree farm.

FILM DIRECTOR: This is great. Yeah. Wow. This is great. So I grew up like a town over from here.

BRI: Oh yeah? Where?

FILM DIRECTOR: Hebron. *(Pronounced HE-brin)*

BRI: Right, Hebron.

FILM DIRECTOR: And I'm trying to use as many local locations as possible.

BRI: You do look familiar.

FILM DIRECTOR: We played soccer against you. I was midfield.

BRI: Right. Yeah. Your goalie was incredible.

FILM DIRECTOR: I know. We still always lost but not by as much as we would have.

BRI: You still play?

FILM DIRECTOR: No, no. I don't.

BRI: I was never very good at running. So you're making a film.

FILM DIRECTOR: Yeah, you know. That's what I do. And they're willing to give me a chance to scout locations out here instead of doing it all of it in a studio, which I appreciate.

BRI: And you want to film here.

FILM DIRECTOR: If you let me.

BRI: Is it a Christmas movie?

FILM DIRECTOR: Yeah. That's what I do. I mean that's not all I do but I do make a lot of Christmas films.

BRI: I love those movies. I watch them every year. Even the bad ones are still fun. So what's yours about?

FILM DIRECTOR: A busy career woman from the city.

(Enter BUSY CAREER WOMAN.*)*

BUSY CAREER WOMAN: *(On phone)* Hello!

BRI: Which city?

FILM DIRECTOR: It's not important. We'll figure that out later.

BUSY CAREER WOMAN: *(On phone)* We have to reschedule everything! And everyone is gone next week! I don't have time for Christmas! I'm coming back to the office as soon as I take care of this.

BRI: What's her career?

FILM DIRECTOR: I don't know. Architect? Journalist. Real estate? But she always wanted to be a tree doctor.

BUSY CAREER WOMAN: But there was never time. *(On phone)* I'm so busy! Goodbye! I have to call someone else!

FILM DIRECTOR: She comes to this small town to help her grandfather's failing Christmas tree farm.

BRI: My farm isn't failing.

FILM DIRECTOR: No, I know. In the story it is. There's a competing Christmas tree farm.

BRI: Oh. We have a competing garden center.

FILM DIRECTOR: And the other farm is run by a dashing handsome man who chops wood barechested in the snow, you know the type, defines masculinity, all that.

(Enter DASHING HANDSOME MAN.*)*

BRI: Okay. Sure.

DASHING HANDSOME MAN: Smell that fresh air! This is the life.

BRI: Yeah. I like it too!

DASHING HANDSOME MAN: When I'm not running this tree farm, I work at a dog rescue, finding new homes for puppies.

BRI: Yeah, sure. I have other jobs too. And hobbies. I like bowling sometimes at the casino. Or Phil and I will play pool.

DASHING HANDSOME MAN: I know how to relax. There's no point in being busy all the time. Life passes you by when you can't stop and smell the pine needles.

BRI: That's actually a Balsam Fir.

DASHING HANDSOME MAN: I know that.

FILM DIRECTOR: And so they're both competing for customers. And there's a meet cute at the local cafe. His rescue dog jumps up on her and spills her coffee all over her.

Busy Career Woman: *(Acting as if dog jumping on her and spilling her coffee)* Oh! My coffee! Who let that mutt in here?

Dashing Handsome Man: I'm sorry, lady.

Film Director: Their eyes meet.

Busy Career Woman: *(Smitten)* Oh!

Dashing Handsome Man: She's a rescue. Sometimes she's not well behaved. Let me buy you another coffee.

Busy Career Woman: That's not necessary.

Dashing Handsome Man: I insist.

Busy Career Woman: Well, if you insist! I am addicted to caffeine, so…

Film Director: And they talk and they talk and they flirt. Build a snowman. Go ice skating. Go on a sleigh ride.

Bri: We actually do that here.

Film Director: But they don't know that they're in competition with each other until they're in too deep.

Bri: Got it. But. What if you do something else?

Film Director: Like what kind of something else?

*(*Dashing Handsome Man *and* Busy Career Woman *stop flirting and stand waiting.)*

Dashing Handsome Man: I can do all sorts of stuff. I'm very versatile.

Busy Career Woman: Me too. I studied at Juilliard.

Bri: Well what about lots of different love stories that all take place at a Christmas Tree Farm.

Dashing Handsome Man: There's still a lead though, right?

Film Director: I don't hate it. Like what kind of stories?

BRI: Like a meet cute between two people who want the same tree.

FILM DIRECTOR: Okay.

BRI: Or this young couple that comes at night to look at the stars.

FILM DIRECTOR: Sure.

BRI: Or there are these novelists.

FILM DIRECTOR: What do you mean?

BRI: They're having a hard time. And there's these four Santas. And an Elf.

FILM DIRECTOR: Okay.

BRI: There's a thing usually with the mayor.

FILM DIRECTOR: Sure. Or the filmmaker who wants to film something on a Christmas tree farm and tries to talk the owner into it.

BRI: Okay. And there's like this angel.

FILM DIRECTOR: There's an angel?

BRI: People keep seeing this angel.

FILM DIRECTOR: Really?

(Angelic music. A light change. ANGEL *shows up in all white with maybe a halo, wings. They are beautiful. A moment while both* BRI *and* FILM DIRECTOR *stare.)*

ANGEL: Hi. You looking at my costume? I'm in a play at the church. I found the tree I want. Could you cut it down for me?

(Lights go back to normal.)

BRI: Sure. Sure. I'll be right with you.

BUSY CAREER WOMAN: So do you need us or should we go?

(Exit ANGEL*)*

DASHING HANDSOME MAN: *(To* BUSY CAREER WOMAN*)* Let's go. I know a place near here with hot toddies. You like hot toddies?

BUSY CAREER WOMAN: I do.

*(*DASHING HANDSOME MAN *and* BUSY CAREER WOMAN *walk off arm-in-arm)*

BRI: Or high school sweethearts who see each other for the first time after a long time has passed.

FILM DIRECTOR: I really like that.

BRI: Their lockers were next to each other all through high school.

*(*FILM DIRECTOR *takes notes.)*

NINE
"High School Sweethearts"

BRI: And then Palmer thinks *(he/she/they)* sees an angel on the other side of the tree.

(We hear the angel music and see the angel lighting again.)

BRI: —but it was just *(his/her/their)* high school sweetheart, Quinn.

(Angel lights and music ends. They see each other.)

PALMER: Wow, hey.

QUINN: Hi.

PALMER: Is that you?

QUINN: I think so.

PALMER: I did not expect to see you on the other side of this tree just now.

QUINN: I know. I haven't seen you since—

PALMER: Not since high school.

QUINN: Whoa! Really? That can't be true.

PALMER: It's true.

QUINN: You might be right.

BRI: Their lockers were right next to each other for four years.

(Light change. As if PALMER *and* QUINN *are in high school at their lockers.)*

PALMER: Hey.

QUINN: Hi.

PALMER: Fourth period.

QUINN: Yeah. Whatta ya gonna do.

PALMER: Got to get my books again I guess.

(A new day)

PALMER: Hey.

QUINN: Hi.

(A new day)

PALMER: Hey.

QUINN: Hi.

(A new day)

PALMER: Hey.

QUINN: Hi.

BRI: Over and over and over and over. Sometimes they confided in each other.

QUINN: I hate her so much.

PALMER: I know. She's the worst.

BRI: But they rarely had any classes together. It was all between classes in two minute increments.

PALMER: Hey.

QUINN: Hi.

PALMER: *(Joking)* Long time no see.

QUINN: What ya been doin'?

PALMER: This and that. You?

QUINN: That and this. School.

BRI: One day [he/she/they] reached down and accidentally touched [his/her/their] hand. They both laughed it off.

PALMER: Sorry.

QUINN: It's fine. Next time buy me dinner first.

PALMER: You want me to?

QUINN: What?

PALMER: Nothing. *(A new day)* Hey!

QUINN: Hi.

BRI: And then they were in chemistry together their senior year and there was a lot of chemistry between them.

PALMER: Hey lab partner.

QUINN: Hi lab partner.

PALMER: I guess we should make those charts.

QUINN: Yeah.

PALMER: And graphs.

QUINN: Yeah. You free after school today?

PALMER: Yeah. Your place or mine? Sorry that sounded…

QUINN: What?

PALMER: Ha! Heh! Nothing.

QUINN: Come to my house.

PALMER: Yeah, okay, yeah.

BRI: Poring over the data, they had their first kiss.

PALMER: Oh!

QUINN: Wow.

BRI: What followed was something they considered a torrid affair.

PALMER: I missed you.

QUINN: I missed you more.

PALMER: I like you.

QUINN: I like you more.

PALMER: I love you.

QUINN: I love you more.

BRI: When they broke up, a month before graduation it felt like the adult thing to do.

PALMER: We'll be at college in different parts of the country.

QUINN: Yeah. Long distance never works.

BRI: Which was a thing they heard someone say and they both believed it.

QUINN: This way is for the best.

PALMER: It hurts now but it'll be better in the long run.

QUINN: Our lives diverge here.

PALMER: We're so mature the way we're handing this.

BRI: Of course there were a lot of tears all the same. They got back together and broke up twice more in the next two weeks. Each day they saw each other at their lockers.

PALMER: Hey. *(Stifling a sob)*

QUINN: Hi. *(Stifling a sob)*

BRI: And then they graduated. It was a hard summer. They decided to stop all communication. And then colleges started and they didn't stay in touch. And then while they were at school, Palmer's family moved away. And from then on, home was a different place. So they never ran into each other on Christmases. Until now.

QUINN: You look good.

PALMER: You do.

QUINN: No I don't. I'm old now.

PALMER: You're not old because I'm not. And you do look good.

QUINN: Well all right. How are you? I've thought about you.

PALMER: You have?

QUINN: Now and then. Not all the time. Don't get a big head.

PALMER: Me too. I think about you too. You never forget your first love.

QUINN: Is that what I was?

PALMER: Maybe I shouldn't have said that.

QUINN: You were my first love too.

PALMER: Wow, it's… It's just real good to see you. I've tried to find out about you but you're not on the—

QUINN: Yeah I never really liked it.

PALMER: And I guess I don't talk to anyone who talks to you.

QUINN: Who do you talk to?

PALMER: Joe. Nicole. Karianne.

QUINN: Oh. Good. I talk to James still.

PALMER: Sure. How is James?

QUINN: Good.

PALMER: How are you?

QUINN: Good. You?

PALMER: Good. You uh, married? Have kids?

QUINN: Divorced. No kids. You?

PALMER: No.

QUINN: Oh.

PALMER: No kids. I wanted some.

QUINN: I did too. So you're single.

PALMER: I am. Are you?

QUINN: I am. You live here now?

PALMER: Moved back. Last year. From Glastonbury.

QUINN: Oh.

PALMER: Taking care of my mom. She wanted to be here. Reminds her of better times.

QUINN: Me too. How is Shirley?

PALMER: She's okay. She asked about you, actually.

QUINN: No!

PALMER: She did. She thinks we should have ended up together.

QUINN: Does she? Yeah. I should have kept in touch.

PALMER: I should have.

QUINN: But then I didn't know who you became. I wasn't sure who I became.

PALMER: You look the same.

QUINN: You do.

PALMER: Did we make a mistake, breaking up all those years ago?

QUINN: I don't know. Did we? I don't know. No sense wondering what could have been. What happened

happened and we can't take it back. And we were free to live our lives, study, work, fall in and out of love.

PALMER: I don't know if I ever loved anyone as much as I loved you.

QUINN: Me too.

PALMER: So, can I buy you dinner?

QUINN: I'd love that. First I need a tree.

PALMER: I do too. My mom wants a very small one.

QUINN: I'll help you look.

BRI: Their fingers accidentally touch.

PALMER: Oh.

BRI: And then they are holding hands. Decades have passed but it seems natural—normal—like only a few minutes ago they were seeing each other again between classes.

PALMER: Hey.

QUINN: Hi.

TEN
"Garden Center Owner"

BRI: And then the competition shows up. Drew, who I grew up with and who owns the garden center now, drives over just to inspect my branches, stroll between my rows.

DREW: (*Narrating*) The farm is empty of people. The wind whistles through the trees.

BRI: Stop that. Don't do that. This is my place.

DREW: Bri looks at me with a new sense of respect.

BRI: I do not.

DREW: The winter cold surrounds us. The wind whips at us, mercilessly.

BRI: I'm actually not that cold.

DREW: Yeah. Quiet here. I thought you'd have the horses hooked up to the sleigh.

BRI: We do that Saturday. We have a Santa coming. Floyd will do sleigh rides. Verna's making her hot chocolate.

DREW: We sold sixteen hundred trees so far.

BRI: That's good.

DREW: I think we sold more last year at this time.

BRI: What can I do for you? You run out of trees?

DREW: We ran out of trees. I mean not completely. There are a few. But people are showing up, looking at the trees and then leaving.

BRI: Like I said, we have enough acreage that we could be your supplier.

DREW: I know.

BRI: Every year I say this.

DREW: They're cheaper from my supplier. If I get them all from you, I mark them up and then people come here instead because yours are cheaper.

BRI: You want me to mark mine up too?

DREW: I mean, yeah.

BRI: I'm not going to do that. I'll just wait until this time of year most years when you have to come here and buy from me and sell at a loss or else bump up your price. How many you want?

DREW: I guess fifty. Different sizes.

BRI: I'll get the chainsaw.

DREW: Thanks. I appreciate it.

BRI: Don't mention it.

DREW: Before you uh grab the saw—

BRI: What's up?

DREW: No no no. Nevermind.

BRI: Should I get the chainsaw then?

DREW: How many years have I been coming here?

BRI: Probably most years since you opened. There are trucking problems or supply issues.

DREW: But we've known each other since what? Fourth grade?

BRI: Is that when you moved to town?

DREW: Yeah. You know what? Forget it.

BRI: I know what this is. People get ideas when they come here. In fact I've always meant to ask you if it's like that at the garden center too.

DREW: Like what?

BRI: If you see a lot of people falling in and out of love on a daily basis.

DREW: You think I'm in love with you?

BRI: I don't know. Are you?

DREW: Bri, sometimes you're infuriating.

BRI: Always have been. That doesn't really answer my question though.

DREW: Forget it.

BRI: No, what were you going to say?

DREW: Just start up the chainsaw so I don't have to hear you anymore.

BRI: Don't be like that.

DREW: You don't know me.

BRI: But I do, kind of. Or I did. I knew you when you were ten. We were friends when we were fifteen. You and me and Terry. All through high school we were inseparable.

(Enter TERRY *who isn't really there, probably wears pale or white clothes like a ghost or angel. Leather jacket also possible.* BRI *hands the zippo to* TERRY *who fiddles with it.)*

TERRY: All right film club, whose turn is it next?

BRI: It's mine. I don't think we see enough French New Wave.

DREW: No! No! Truffaut is a fraud.

BRI: I mean that's a little…

DREW: If I have to sit through another—

BRI: But it's my turn.

DREW: I'll give you two turns if I don't have to sit though Truffaut again.

BRI: Godard then.

DREW: Are you serious? What's wrong with film noir, or spaghetti western? I'll watch Hitchcock even.

BRI: *(To DREW)* Mmm hmm. What are you proposing?

DREW: Well it's around Christmas so maybe we should watch a Christmas film.

BRI: We can wear Santa hats while we watch Truffaut.

DREW: If I have to watch another one of those films, I'll die.

TERRY: It's just two hours of your life. Let's just watch what Bri wants to watch.

BRI: Thank you.

DREW: Fine.

TERRY: And then when it's your turn we'll watch your Christmas horror film.

DREW: Terry was so cool.

BRI: So cool.

DREW: Remember that leather jacket?

BRI: How could I forget?

DREW: You ever ride on the back of *(his/her/their)* motorcycle?

BRI: Sure. Of course.

DREW: The wind whipping against your skin. Exciting, maybe a little scary sometimes.

TERRY: Hold on tight—

DREW: — *(he/she/they)* would say.

BRI: I held on tight.

DREW: Me too.

BRI: That motorcycle.

DREW: There's nothing we could do.

BRI: It wasn't even slippery out. It wasn't raining or snowing. No ice on the ground. Just one of those things. Just a mistake. Off balance for a second or— well I wasn't there.

DREW: I wasn't there either.

BRI: He slid under a truck and never came back out. And it was hard for me to look at you for a while after.

DREW: I avoided you too.

BRI: I guess I wanted to move on, but I was mourning.

DREW: Film club disbanded. Terry was the one holding us together.

BRI: I didn't get close to anyone for years after.

DREW: Sure.

BRI: I still remember what you said at the funeral.

DREW: "Terry was who we all wanted to be."

TERRY: That's nice.

BRI: I see *(him/her/them)* sometimes. Out here at night. Once in a while.

DREW: I don't believe in all that.

BRI: I know you don't. That's why you've never seen *(him/her/them)*.

DREW: What did *(he/she/they)* look like?

BRI: The same. Maybe a little older. Sometimes I feel like I hear *(his/her/their)* voice in the wind.

DREW: It's so windy here.

TERRY: *(Playing with his lighter)* Be grateful you're still around. You get to feel the wind chafe your skin. Be grateful for everything. Even minor irritations—when you're on hold with the insurance company or waiting in line at the post office, how lucky you are to be alive to be annoyed by it all.

(Angel lighting. Distant angelic sound. TERRY *hands the lighter back to* BRI. *She looks at it. Exit* TERRY*)*

BRI: I almost reached out to you a couple times. Over the years. To say hi or suggest coffee.

DREW: Why didn't you?

BRI: I don't know. And then years flew by. We both moved away and then moved back. Different lives. We were close, though, once, weren't we?

DREW: We were. And if Terry hadn't died, maybe…

BRI: Maybe. *(Beat.)* I'm going to go get the chainsaw.

DREW: Thanks.

ELEVEN
"The Perfect Tree"

(Enter J.)

Bri: It's Friday and J is on a mission.

J: Bri, I'm looking for the perfect tree.

Bri: Oh yeah?

J: Because if I can find the perfect tree maybe she can see I'm someone who can do things well and she will see the value in me and leave that idiot for me.

Bri: Whoa I was not expecting that last part. I'm not sure that's how the world works.

J: It is how the world works. I know. I understand about love. I've read about it and watched all the movies. He doesn't understand about love so she will leave him eventually. I mean, she has to, right?

Bri: Well…

J: I understand the world is unjust but someone like that won't stay with someone like that, right? I'm not saying he doesn't have anything going for him. He's funny sometimes and good looking, I guess. He's a moron though. I mean I think that's clear to everyone. And Jasmine, she's perfect. Okay, I know people aren't really perfect and I know that means she's not really perfect either. But she's nice to everyone and cares about everyone. It's not just that she's beautiful. I mean she is beautiful. It's clear she's beautiful. Stunningly beautiful so much that you could fall apart just being near her. But also she'll smile at you. At everyone she smiles and is kind. Just like a good person who wants the best for everyone, right? And I know he's my older brother.

Bri: Wait, hold on a second— She's with your older brother?

J: But he doesn't love her. And maybe she doesn't love me yet but there's still time. I'm going to become amazing. Just you wait. I will accomplish things.

BRI: What kind of things?

J: I'm not sure yet but like I'm full of potential and I can figure things out. Everyone knows that. And maybe I'll invent a better jello. Or maybe I'll become a great explorer. There's still time for me to figure it out. But she needs to leave him today. He's toxic poisoned diseased trash.

BRI: Really?

J: He's a cancer. And the sooner she's rid of him, the better. She will be happier, much happier after she dumps him and she doesn't even have to start with me right away. I understand mourning periods.

BRI: You know it might not work out. Even if she—

J: No, I know.

BRI: Even if you do everything right. Even if you find the perfect tree. The reason why some people click and others don't is really hard to understand. I mean I think science can't explain. They'll say pheromones or something but it's also the way people's brains work and what people appreciate in other people. She might even like the things in your brother that you hate about him.

J: No, I know.

BRI: And things happen when they happen. She could dump him tomorrow, sure but that might never happen. Even if they aren't right for each other, they could stay together forever because that's the way it is sometimes.

J: Well, okay, but—

BRI: And also I'm saying. She doesn't owe you her love.

J: No, I know.

Bri: And even if she never sees the amazing things about you, that doesn't mean there aren't amazing things about you someone else will see.

J: Thanks. That's nice of you to say. I do think if I can get the perfect tree and surprise her with it, it could work.

Bri: Well look. I sell trees so I'm not going to discourage you from buying a tree and I think I have at least a few perfect trees here.

J: That's all I'm saying.

Bri: But like maybe she wants jewelry or flowers or something thoughtful that shows you listen to her. Like something she specifically wants.

J: She really likes Christmas trees and Christmas. She's kind of obsessed. Like she talks about the perfect height of a tree and like the ones with needles that aren't sharp and blue green instead of yellow green and full but not so full you can't tell it's a real tree. And also with no mice living in it. She didn't like that when that happened one year.

Bri: And you'll just ring the doorbell and say "Merry Christmas I brought you a tree?"

J: Yeah. You think it's a bad idea?

Bri: Yes. I think it's a bad idea. I mean people like to pick out their own trees.

J: Okay.

Bri: And you know, it's not a normal surprise. I think it's the wrong kind of surprise.

J: In romantic comedies, there's always a big gesture.

Bri: Yeah but in real life I think most people like small gestures better most of the time. It gets embarrassing if people sing to you in public or propose in front of a stadium full of people.

J: I hear you.

BRI: Okay.

J: But I'm going to do it anyway. I think maybe some people like that sort of thing and maybe she's maybe one of those people.

BRI: Well I guess… Okay. You want a tree for your house too?

J: No, I'm going to let my brother do that and he'll mess it up and that will help.

BRI: Okay, well… okay. Good luck I guess. But also, maybe, don't get your hopes up?

J: What's the world without hope?

BRI: No, yeah, I agree, but—

J: Just show me some trees please.

BRI: Yeah, for sure. You can call me if it goes bad. I'll be a shoulder for you if you want and also call me if it goes well too because I'd like to know that. Maybe this tree gift surprise thing is a new marketing angle I haven't considered.

J: All right. For sure. I'll let you know.

(Sound of doorbell)

TWELVE
"Tree Lighting"

BRI: And then the mayor comes to show me her speech for the tree lighting.

DANA: I want to keep it short but I also want to say everything that needs to be said.

BRI: You don't need me for this.

DANA: Bri, I appreciate your input. It was really helpful last year.

BRI: Who am I to tell you what to do?

DANA: You know who you are. Please?

(DANA *shows it to* BRI.)

BRI: Yeah, okay. Let me see. Oh yeah this is good. Maybe take out the skating pond part.

DANA: You think?

BRI: I don't think you need it. And it's nice to thank everyone but it gets boring when the list is so long. Maybe save that for next time.

DANA: But they want me to thank them.

BRI: I know but you should thank everybody really and you can't thank everybody. Unless you just say, "Thank you, everybody."

DANA: But that's not the same.

BRI: No but they didn't come for that. And most people don't want to be reminded that they aren't on your list of important people to thank.

DANA: Oh. I get that.

BRI: The more this could be about our community, the better I think. Because that's what's really important. All of us.

DANA: That's nicely put. Should I wear the sweater that lights up?

BRI: I think you should wear that everyday, Dana. How's the family?

DANA: Good. Mostly good. You know. Dan wants to coach Danielle's hockey team but she doesn't want him to.

BRI: Sure.

DANA: How about you?

BRI: Me?

DANA: I worry about you. I worry that you're lonely.

BRI: Some people like being alone though.

DANA: Are you one of those people?

BRI: Not everybody gets what they want.

DANA: Well let me know if you ever change your mind. I'm sure there's someone I could set you up with. I know a lot of people, you know.

BRI: I know.

DANA: And you're pretty great.

BRI: I'll think about it. Can you read the beginning of your speech to me?

DANA: Thank you all for coming. I want to speak in support of spectacle. I want to talk about the importance of appreciating everyday beauty in the world.

(*While* DANA *speaks, the rest of the cast enters. Lights change to tree lighting ceremony. If it's a small cast, have them dress as whichever character they want. Or as the carolers from the beginning. It would be great if someone was dressed as an angel like from a church play. The cast hums* Jingle Bells *low over the next part.*)

BRI: In the crowd at the Tree Lighting ceremony I see the meet cute, who are still cute and the novelists are there talking to other people and the stargazers have come to see the Christmas lights and two of the Santas are sharing one cider and the film director is there filming it and the high school sweethearts are holding hands and—

J: Hi.

BRI: Did the surprise tree work?

J: No. But maybe. I think I'm making headway.

BRI: Okay well I wish for you whatever is supposed to happen.

J: Right back atcha.

BRI: —and Drew who runs the garden center is there too and *(he/she/they)* looks at me and I look at *(him/her/them)*

BRI: Hi.

DREW: Hi. Listen I've been a fool.

BRI: Oh. Sure. I mean—

DREW: I should totally just buy your trees. I'm going to do that from now on. If you have enough, that is.

BRI: We have enough.

DREW: Buy local right?

BRI: Right. And maybe I could raise my prices just a little so that they're somewhere near yours.

DREW: And listen, about you and me…

BRI: Yeah?

DREW: You're not wrong. I just. I move slow.

BRI: I don't mind that. I like a slow pace of life.

DREW: You do?

BRI: I mean I live here.

DREW: Yeah. So. Does that mean it'd be something you'd be into, us? We?

BRI: I think so. If you are. We should try it.

DREW: Yeah.

BRI: You got to try stuff.

DREW: You do. We could see a film.

BRI: I'd like that. If we can agree on something to see.

DREW: I'm more agreeable nowadays. In fact, I think Truffaut is actually pretty—

DANA: Thank you all for coming. I want to speak in support of spectacle. I want to talk about the importance of appreciating everyday beauty in the world. I know to some people it feels like the holiday season lasts for months and months. The music starts and the lights go up and we are asked to have a generous joyous spirit for weeks and weeks. And I know that's difficult to sustain. Also I know that people have lost loved ones and it's hard to go through this time of year without them because you remember sledding together or making cookies or watching movies, putting up lights, making egg nog. It's different for everyone but I'm always delighted to see so many of you here each year. Thanks for braving the cold and the ice to watch me plug in some lights. I see you, all of you. Those of you struggling with money and with children and with jobs and broken cars and cancers and sprained ankles and depression and addiction and the other things that just come from being alive. I see you and I thank you for being here and being alive with me.

(She flips a switch and all the trees onstage light up. It's beautiful. Then DANA opens her coat to reveal her light up sweater. An Angelic sound and light accompanies the sweater reveal.)

BRI: That was real nice.

DANA: Thanks.

BRI: Even better than last year I think.

DANA: Thanks.

BRI: I want you to meet someone. Do you know Drew?

DANA: Hi Drew. Good to see you.

BRI: *(To audience)* Well that's it. Thanks for coming. Have a happy holiday. And a good New Year too. And don't forget to tip your Christmas tree farmer.

(It starts snowing—or this could also happen earlier as we shift to the lighting for the tree lighting. The carolers, really the whole cast sings a Christmas carol for the curtain call. We Wish You a Merry Christmas, possibly. Something upbeat like that. Don't sing the whole song.)

(Blackout)

END OF PLAY